SA
MU

SAINT MUNGO

ALSO KNOWN AS KENTIGERN

BY JOCELINUS, A MONK OF FURNESS

EDITED AND PRESENTED
BY IAIN MACDONALD

FLORIS BOOKS

First published in 1993 by Floris Books

The publisher acknowledges subsidy from the
Scottish Arts Council towards the publication
of this volume.

British Library CIP Data available

ISBN 0-86315-166-3

Printed in Great Britain
by BPCC Wheatons Ltd, Exeter

Contents

Introduction

St Mungo (Kentigern) lived during the half century AD 560 to 612. His sphere of work was the south of Scotland and the north west of England during a time when historical records are very scanty.

In the face of the Gothic and Germanic attacks on the Roman Empire, the Romans had withdrawn from Britain in 410 leaving the Britons exposed to on-slaughts from nearly all sides. Nevertheless in the year 560 the Britons still vigorously maintained a presence in the region of Cambria. The Cambrian kingdoms of the Britons comprised Strathclyde, Galloway, Cumbria and the Lothians.

North of the Forth and Clyde lived the Picts. There were however also southern Pictish settlements mingled with the Britons in the Lothians and southern uplands of Scotland.

About the year 450 the Scoti (or Gaels from Ireland) had established their kingdom of Dalriada in Argyll. One hundred years later (559) these Scoti were defeated by Brude MacMaelchon, king of the northern Picts, and their kingdom was subjected to the Pictish king. Later under their energetic King Aidan (574-605), aided by

St Columba, the Scots of Dalriada reasserted their independence.

The main antagonists of the Britons of Cambria however were the Angles. These Germanic marauders, coming from Denmark, were raiding the east coast of Britain as early as Roman times. In 547 under their formidable chief Ida, the Angles had firmly established themselves in Bernicia (Northumberland) and built their fortress, Bamborough. During the next fifty years, these Angles steadily increased their hold on Bernicia at the expense of the Britons. In 603, during St Kentigern's lifetime, the Angles under their king Aethelfrith defeated a combined army of Britons and Gaels at Degestan in Dumfriesshire.

Thus we see Scotland and northern England divided among four peoples: the Britons, the Picts, the Scots (Gaels) and the Angles. But it would be incorrect to assume that there were distinct boundaries between these peoples. There is evidence of intermigration and intermarriage. In years of strife, clan alliances were formed regardless of nation, and a powerful chief could have a multi-national band of warriors. Other strands of intermingling were fostered by trade and religion.

Despite the withdrawal of the Romans, the Christian Church continued to flourish and extend its influence. St Ninian's foundation in Galloway, the

Candida Casa (431) continued to be a seat of Christian learning. From there evangelization proceeded among the Cambrian Britons and the southern Picts. Nevertheless it would appear that Druidic cults still persisted. In 563 St Columba founded his famous Abbey of Iona, from which he not only worked among his own people, the Gaels of Dalriada, but also travelled among the Britons. Most important of all was his mission to the northern Picts and his conversion of their king, Brude. Throughout all this time, that is during the life of St Kentigern, the Angles remained thoroughly pagan, followers of Wotan, Thor and all the Germanic deities. Their conversion to Christianity was not to come until after the death of St Kentigern when their king, Edwin, married a Christian princess in 616.

Legend, with a few historical handholds, ascribes to this time and to the lands where St Kentigern travelled and worked, the activities of King Arthur and his knights. King Lot of the Lothians features in the tales, and there is a delightful legend which tells that Merlin, the great magician of King Arthur's court, at the end of his life roamed the woods of Drumelzier in Peeblesshire. There St Kentigern found him and baptized him a Christian.

St Kentigern's day is January 13.

The oldest source relating to St Kentigern which has come down to us is a fragment describing the life of his mother, St Theneu, up to his birth. This fragment was written by "a cleric of St Kentigern" at the instance of Herbert, the venerable Bishop of Glasgow. Herbert died in 1164, so this manuscript must have been written before that date.

About the year 1184 Jocelyne, a monk at the Benedictine Abbey of Furness in North Lancashire wrote his Vita Sancti Kentigerni Episcopi et Confessoris. *This work he dedicated to Jocelinus, Bishop of Glasgow during the reign of William I of Scotland (the Lion). Jocelyne's* Vita *exists in two Latin manuscripts.*

The two manuscripts of Jocelyne and that of the anonymous cleric of St Kentigern were carefully collated, edited and translated into English by Alexander Penrose Forbes, Bishop of Brechin, who published them in 1874 in his book, Historians of Scotland *(Vol. 5). The text presented here is edited and abridged from Forbes' translation.*

Of Jocelyne we know no more than what he tells himself in a prologue. Writing six hundred years after the death of St Kentigern he mentions the sources of his story, and in particular "one little volume written in the Scotic dialect." None of these sources has survived.

The life of St Kentigern

Jocelinus begins his account with the colourful story of Kentigern's mother, the unwedded daughter of a pagan king in northern Britain. After being converted to Christianity, she became devoted to the figure of the Virgin Mother and prayed that she could imitate her in all things. On finding herself with child, she believed fervently that her prayer had been answered and swore on oath that she had not had intercourse with any man. Jocelinus is at pains to argue that only "stupid and foolish people" would seriously accept this as a genuine case of a virgin conception. Certainly the girl's father did not, and invoked the old Saxon law by which she must be put to death.

The girl was taken to be cast down from the top of a high hill, and this was done. However she sustained no injury, to the astonishment of the crowd, some of whom concluded that she must be a witch. Finally it was decided to cast her adrift upon the sea in a coracle, and so the king's servants took her far out from the coast and consigned her little craft to the mercy of the waves. Jocelinus continues: Wonderful to relate, that little vessel ploughed the watery breakers and eddies of the waves more quickly than if propelled by a wind that filled the sail, or by the effort of many oarsmen.

The birth of Kentigern and his education by St Servanus. The girl landed at a place called Culenros, where at that time St Servanus dwelt, teaching sacred literature to many boys who were to be trained to the divine service. When she had landed on the shore the pains of approaching childbirth seized her. Raising her eyes, she saw at a distance the ashes of a fire near the shore, which perhaps some shepherds or fishermen had left there. She crawled to the place, and as best she might kindled for herself a fire. But when the dawn began to brighten, the time was accomplished and she brought forth a son.

Now, at the same hour, while St Servanus was at prayer after Mass, he heard the companies of the angels chanting praises on high. On the clerics being astonished at this, and demanding what had happened, he told them all in order the whole matter, and the hymnings of the angels. But there were in the neighbourhood shepherds keeping watch over the flocks. And going forth in the early morning, they beheld a fire lighted close at hand,

and coming with haste found the young woman with the child wrapped in rags, and lying in the open air. Moved by pity, they took care of them by increasing the fire and supplying food and other necessaries; and bringing them in and presenting them to St Servanus, related the matter from the beginning.

On hearing this, and seeing the little boy, the mouth of the blessed old man was filled with spiritual laughter, and his heart with joy. Wherefore in the language of his country he exclaimed: "Mochohe, Mochohe," which in Latin means Care mi, Care mi, adding: "Blessed art thou that hast come in the name of the Lord." He therefore took them to himself, and nourished and educated them as if they were his own pledges. After certain days had passed he baptized them and anointed them with the sacred chrism, calling the mother Taneu, and the child Kyentyern, which means, "The Capital Lord."

The child grew, and the grace of God was in him. But when the age of intelligence and the time for learning arrived, Servanus handed him over to be trained in letters. Nor was he disappointed, seeing that the boy richly responded to his training.

All his gifts of grace were gilded by a worthy life, and therefore beyond all his companions he was precious and amiable in the eyes of the holy old man, who for this reason used to call him in the language of his country, "Munghu, " which in Latin means *carissimus amicus,* and by this name even to the present time the common people frequently call him, and invoke him in their need.

Of the little bird that was killed, and then restored to life by Kentigern.

The fellow-pupils of St Kentigern, seeing that he was loved beyond the rest by their master and spiritual father, hated him, and were unable either in public or private to say anything peaceable to him. Hence in many ways they intrigued against him.

Now a little bird which is called the redbreast, was accustomed to receive its daily food from the hand of Servanus, and showed itself tame and domesticated to him. Sometimes even it perched upon his head, or face, or shoulder, or bosom; sometimes it was with him when he read or prayed, and by the flapping of its wings, or by the sound of its voice or by some little gesture, it showed the love it had for him.

On a certain day, when the saint entered his

oratory, the boys began to play with the little bird, and while they handled it among them and sought to snatch it from each other, it got destroyed in their hands, and its head was torn from the body.

On this play became sorrow, and they already in imagination felt the blows of the rods. Having taken counsel among themselves, they laid the blame on the boy Kentigern. The old man took very ill the death of the bird, and threatened a severe vengeance on its destroyer. The boys therefore rejoiced, thinking that they had escaped, and had turned on Kentigern the punishment due to them and diminished the friendship which Servanus entertained for him.

When Kentigern learned this, taking the bird in his hands, and putting the head upon the body, he signed it with the sign of the cross, and lifted up his hands in prayer. Straightaway the bird revived, and flew forth with joy to meet the holy old man as he returned from the church. On seeing this prodigy the heart of the old man rejoiced in the Lord. By this remarkable sign did the Lord mark out Kentigern as his own, and announced him who later, in manifold ways, He made still more distinguished by wonders.

How St Kentigern departed secretly from St Servanus,
and what sort of a miracle was wrought at his departing.
When the sanctity of St Kentigern shone forth,
illustrated by such remarkable signs, his rivals
sowed the seed of greater hatred against the saint
of God. The boy knew that the measure of their
malice against himself was filled up. He forthwith
proposed to leave the place, that he might forsake
the company of those who hated and envied him,
and also prudently avoid vainglory.

He therefore retreated secretly from the place,
and journeying, he arrived where the river called
Mallena, overflowing its banks when the tide
comes in, took away all hope of crossing. But the
kind and mighty Lord, who divided the Red Sea
and led the people of Israel through dry-shod,
now with the same mighty hand divided the river
Mallena, so that Kentigern might cross on dry
ground. Then the tide flowing back in a very
wonderful way, the waters both of the sea and of
the river stood as walls on his right hand and on
his left. After that, crossing a little arm of the sea,
near a bridge which by the inhabitants is called
the Pons Servani, on looking back to the bank he
saw that the waters now flowed back and filled
the channel.

And behold St Servanus, supporting his aged limbs with a staff, having followed in pursuit of the fugitive, stood above the bank, and beckoning with his hand, he cried out lamenting: "Alas, my dearest son, light of mine eyes, staff of mine old age! Wherefore dost thou desert me?"

Kentigern, moved with these words of the aged man, melting into tears replied: "Thou seest, my father, that what is done is according to the divine will."

Then said the old man: "I pray thee, that by thy intercession, I may reach thee dry-shod, so that to the evening of my days I may be thy companion."

Then again Kentigern, weeping copiously, replied: "Return, I pray thee, my father, to thine own people, that in thy holy presence they may be trained in sacred doctrine, guided by thine example. But I, destined to the work of the ministry, will go forth to that which He sent me, who separated me from my mother's womb, and called me by His grace."

Having said this, and having blessed each other, they were divided and never looked in each other's face again in this world. For Servanus, returning home, awaited in a good old age the day of his call, and thus growing old and being gathered to the holy fathers, he rested in the Lord.

Of the sick man who prayed that before his death he should see St Kentigern.

There was a man of venerable life, Fregus by name, tormented by a long sickness, who lived in a town called Kernach, detained upon the bed of pain. Fregus, with firm faith and frequent prayers, besought of the Lord that he might see Kentigern, the servant of the Lord Christ, and received a promise from the Holy Ghost that he should not see death till he had seen him.

And when Kentigern had come to the habitation of the holy sick man, and knocked at the door, the sick man from within exclaimed, saying: "Open the gates, for the Lord is with us." And when he had seen him he rejoiced and blessed the Lord, and said: "Lord, now lettest Thou Thy servant depart in peace, according to Thy word."

Then, by the advice of holy Kentigern, he gave to the poor all the worldly substance he possessed, and, after making a pure confession, he was anointed with the oil of remission, and purified with the sacrament of the life-giving Body and Blood of the Lord. Then he commended his spirit into the hands of the Lord, and with eyes and hands lifted up to heaven, he expired during the words of prayer.

Of the election of St Kentigern, and his consecration as bishop of Glasgow.

Then, by divine prompting, the king and clergy of the Cambrian region, with other Christians, came together, and after taking into consideration what was to be done to restore the good estate of the Church, which was wellnigh destroyed, they with one consent approached St Kentigern, and elected him, in spite of his many remonstrances and strong resistance, to be the shepherd and bishop of their souls.

St Kentigern established his cathedral seat in a town called Glesgu, which is, interpreted, The Dear Family, and is now called Glasgow. Moreover, the diocese of that episcopate was extended to the limits of the Cambrian kingdom, which reached from sea to sea, like the rampart once built by the Emperor Severus. This rampart afterwards, by the assistance of the Roman Legion, in order to keep off the incursions of the Picts, gave way to a wall built in the same place, eight feet in breadth and twelve feet in height; it reaches as far

as the Flumen Fordense, and separates Scotia from
Anglia.

Now this Cambrian region had once, with all
Britain, accepted the Christian faith in the time
of Pope Eleutherius, when Lucius was king; but
in consequence of the pagans from time to time
infesting the island, the islanders had cast away the
faith which they had received. Many were not yet
baptized. Many were stained by the contagion
of heresy. Many, in name only Christians, were
plunged in the slough of vice of all sorts; the
greatest part of them had been taught by the
ministry of men who were unskilled and ignorant
of the law of God. Thus all the provincials required the counsel of a good pastor.

*How St Kentigern conducted himself in the episcopate;
how he lived and how he taught; and how he deported
himself both openly and in private.*
The saint of God, after accepting the episcopal
dignity, sought to exercise greater humility and
austerity than before in his food, his dress, in
watchings, in his hard couches, and in the morti-
fication of his body.

And that I may in brief describe his whole life,
from the time of his ordination, which took place

in the twenty-fifth year of his age, until the
extreme term of his life, which lasted the space
of one hundred and sixty years: When he broke
his fast after three days, or oftener after four days,
he revived rather than recruited his body by
tasting the cheapest and lightest foods, such as
bread and milk, and cheese and butter and con-
diments. He abstained entirely from flesh and
from blood, and from wine, and from all that
could inebriate. If, however, at any time it happened that he was on a journey, or dining with
the king, he tempered the usual rigour of his
abstinence. Afterwards, when he returned home,
punishing in himself that which he regarded as a
gross crime, he increased his abstinence.

Of the mode of dress of St Kentigern.
He used the roughest hair-cloth next the skin,
then a garment of leather made of the skin of the
goats, then a cowl like a fisherman's bound on
him, above which, clothed in a white alb, he
always wore a stole over his shoulders. He bore a
pastoral staff; not rounded and gilded and gem-
med, as may be seen nowadays, but of simple
wood, and merely bent. He had in his hand the
Manual-book, always ready to exercise his min-

istry, whenever necessity or reason demanded. And so by the whiteness of his dress he expressed the purity of his inner life, and avoided vainglory.

Of the couch of St Kentigern, and his vigils, and his bath in cold water.

What shall I say of his bed? I hesitate whether to call it a bed or a tomb. He lay in stone hollowed like a monument, having for his head a stone in place of a pillow, like another Jacob. Throwing in a few ashes, and taking off his sackcloth, he shook off his drowsiness rather by tasting than taking sleep. When he had taken a moderate portion of sleep, he arose in the night, at the beginning of his vigils, and poured forth his soul like water in the sight of the Lord his God.

And so with psalms, and hymns, and spiritual songs, celebrating the Lord's night-watches, he exulted in God his Saviour, and was joyful in Him until the second cock-crowing; then, entering upon a fiercer conflict with that great and malignant dragon that, according to the prophet, lies in the midst of his rivers, he used to strip himself of his clothes, and naked, he plunged into the rapid and cold water. Then, as the hart desires the water brooks, so his soul desired and thirsted for God, the living water; and there, in cold and nakedness, with his eyes and hands lifted up to heaven, he chanted on end the whole Psalter.

Of St Kentigern's way of speaking.

In speaking, he was able to control his spirit, and he learned to set a watch before his mouth and to keep the door of his lips, that he might guide his words with discretion. Nor did any one of his words fall lightly to the ground, nor was the word he spoke given to the winds, nor did it return to him in vain. Wherefore he spoke in weight, number, and measure, as the necessary occasion demanded, for his speech was flavoured with salt, suited to every age and sex.

Yet the saint preached more by his silence than many doctors and rulers do by loud speaking, for his appearance, countenance, gait, and the gesture of his whole body, openly taught discipline, and by certain signs flowing forth, outwardly revealed the purity of the inner man.

Of what a bright countenance Kentigern had.

Holy Kentigern is said to have been of middle stature, rather inclining to tallness, and it is asserted that he was of robust strength, capable of enduring great fatigue in the labours both of body and soul. He was beautiful to look upon, and graceful in form. Having a countenance full of grace and reverence, dove-like eyes, cheeks like the turtle-dove, he attracted the hearts of all who beheld him. His outward cheerfulness was the sign and most faithful interpreter of that inward peace, which flooded all things with a certain contentment of holy joy and exultation, which the Lord bestowed upon him.

How Holy Kentigern, by divine aid, transferred the barns of the king to his own dwelling-place.

A certain tyrant, by name Morken, had ascended the throne of the Cambrian kingdom, whom power, honour, and riches had persuaded to exercise himself in matters which were too high for him. But his heart was as elevated by pride, as it was blinded and contracted by greed. He scorned and despised the life and doctrine of the man of God, in secret slandering, in public resisting him from time to time, putting down his miraculous power to magical illusion, and esteeming as nothing all that he did.

But once upon a time Kentigern, when he wanted supplies to feed the brethren of his monastery, betook himself to the king, gently hinting at his poverty and at that of his people, desiring that out of his abundance he should come to their aid. But Morken continually reviled him who made his petition, and only inflicted injuries on him. Then with blasphemous words he said to him ironically:

"Thou hast often taught others that they who seek the Lord shall want no manner of thing that is good. Thou, therefore, though thou fearest God, and keepest His commandments, art in want of everything, while to me who neither seek the kingdom of God nor righteousness, all prosperous things are added."

But the holy man proved from the testimony of the Holy Scriptures that many just and holy men were afflicted by hunger and want in this life; and that wicked men were exalted by wealth, affluence and high honour. And then with power and clearness he taught that the poor were the patrons of the rich, by whose benefits they are sustained, and that the rich need the support of the poor, as the vines are supported by the elm.

Then the barbarian was unable to resist his wisdom and the Spirit who spoke through him, but in a rage answered:

"If, trusting in thy God, without human hand, thou canst transfer to thy mansion all the corn that is kept in my barns, I yield with a glad mind, and for the future will be devoutly obedient to thy requests."

Saying this he went away joyful, as if by such an answer as this he had made game of the saint. But when evening was come, the holy man, lifting his hands and his eyes to heaven, with many tears, prayed most devoutly to the Lord.

In that very hour the river Clud rose and became swollen in flood; then extending beyond its banks and surrounding the barns of the king, it drew them into its channel, and transported them to dry land at a place called Mellingdenor, where the saint was at that time dwelling. Straightaway the river ceased from its fury, and controlled within itself the surging waves. There the barns were found whole and uninjured, and not a sheaf, not a single blade, appeared to be wetted.

How King Morken, at the urging of his military follower Cathen, struck St Kentigern with his foot, and with what punishment both were visited.

King Morken though very rich and great in the eyes of men, yet bore ill the loss of his stock of

corn. Therefore his eye being consumed because
of fury, he emitted many reproaches against the
holy bishop, calling him magician and sorcerer,
and he commanded that if ever again he appeared
in his presence he should suffer severely.

The reason for this was that a wicked man
named Cathen, who was the king's confidential
friend, had urged him on to hatred of the bishop,
because the life of the good is usually hateful and
burdensome to the wicked.

But the man of God, wishing by wisdom to
extinguish malice, approached the presence of the
king in the spirit of meekness and, instructing and
warning him after the manner of a most gentle
father, sought to correct the folly of a son. But
the king acquiesced not in the warning words.
Excited by fiercer madness, he rushed upon him,
struck him with his heel, and smote him to the
ground upon his back. But the saint of God, being
raised by the bystanders, bore most patiently both
the hurt and the dishonour, committing his cause
to the vindication of the Supreme Judge, and then
he departed from this sacrilegious king, rejoicing
that he was deemed worthy to suffer for the word
of the Lord.

The instigator of this sacrilege, Cathen, laughing loudly, mounted his horse, and seemingly triumphing over the saint, departed full of joy. He had not gone far when the prancing steed on which he was seated, striking his foot on some stumbling-block, fell down, and his rider, falling backward, broke the neck which he had erected loftily against the servant of the Lord, and expired before the gate of the king his master.

Then a swelling attacked the feet of the king; pain followed the swelling, and then succeeded death; so expiring in the royal town which after him was termed Thorp-morken, he was buried. But the disease was not destroyed or buried in the succession of that family.

After this, for many days Kentigern enjoyed great peace and quiet, living in his own city of Glasgow, and going through his diocese; because the divine vengeance, shown forth upon his persecutors, supplied to others a motive of fear, reverence, love, and obedience towards the saint of God.

How holy Kentigern, avoiding the snares of those who plotted his death, departed from his country and betook himself to St David.

When some time had passed, a generation of

vipers of the kin of King Morken, excited by intense hatred, took counsel together how they might lay hold of Kentigern by craft, and put him to death; but fearing the people, they did not dare to do that evil deed openly, because all held him for a teacher, bishop, and shepherd of their souls, and loved him as an angel of light and peace.

At last, binding themselves together by a solemn oath, they determined that in no way would they fail in the resolve to compass his death. And when the man of God had learnt this, although he could meet force by force, he thought it better for the time to quit the place and to seek elsewhere a richer harvest of souls.

At last, instructed by divine revelation, he journeyed from those regions towards Menevia, where at that time the holy Bishop Dewi [David] was shining forth in his episcopal work.

And when he had come to Karleolum [Carlisle], he heard that many among the mountains were given to idolatry, or ignorant of the divine law. There he turned aside, and converted to the Christian religion many from a strange belief, and others who were erroneous in the faith. He remained some time in a certain thickly planted place, to confirm and comfort in the faith the men that dwelt there, where he erected a cross as the sign of the faith; whence it took the name, in English, of Crosfeld, that is, Crucis Novale.

Turning aside from thence, the saint directed his journey by the sea, and at length he reached St Dewi, and found in him greater works than had been reported by fame. The holy Bishop Dewi rejoiced greatly at the arrival of so great a stranger. With eyes overflowing with tears, and mutually embracing, he received Kentigern as an angel of the Lord, dear to God, and retaining him for a time in his vicinity, honoured him to a wonderful extent.

And when St Kentigern had abode there some time, his fame led him to much familiarity and friendship, not only with the poor, the middle class, and the nobility of that land, but even with King Cathwallain, who reigned in that country. For the king, knowing him to be a holy and righteous man, heard him willingly, and after hearing him, did much which concerned the good of his own soul. And when Kentigern said he would wish to live near, and have the means of building a monastery, the king replied:

"My land is in thy sight: wherever it suiteth thee and seemeth good in thy sight, there build thy monastery. Yet, as it seemeth to me that it is more suitable for thee than any other I assign to thee a place, Nautcharvan, because it aboundeth in everything suited to thy purpose."

The man of God rendered profuse thanks to the king, and chose for his building and habitation that place which had been marked out for him by divine intimation. Then, giving his blessing to the king, he departed: and bidding farewell to St Dewi, he betook himself to the place with a great multitude of disciples who had flocked to him, preferring to lead with him a lowly life in a foreign land to living without him luxuriously in their own.

How St Kentigern, following a boar which led the way, found a fitting place for his monastery.

Thus the most holy Kentigern gave no sound sleep to his eyes, nor quiet rest to his eyelids, until he found a place fit for building a tabernacle to the Lord, the God of Jacob. With a great crowd of his disciples he went round the land exploring the localities, the quality of the air, the richness of the soil, the sufficiency of the meadows, pastures, and woods, and the other things that look to the convenience of a monastery to be erected.

And while they went together over abrupt mountains, hollow valleys, caves of the earth, thickset briers, dark woods, and open glades in the forest, lo and behold, a wild boar from the wood, entirely white, met them, and sometimes advancing a little, and then returning and looking backwards, motioned to the saint and to his companions, with such gesture as he could, to follow him.

On seeing this they wondered and glorified God, who works marvellous things, and things past understanding in His creatures. Then they followed the boar, which preceded them.

When they came to the place which the Lord had predestined for them, the boar halted, and frequently striking the ground with his foot, and making the gesture of tearing up the soil of the little hill that was there with his long tusk, shaking his head repeatedly and grunting, he clearly showed to all that that was the place designed and prepared by God. Now the place is situated on the bank of a river called Elgu, from which to this day, as it is said, the town takes its name.

Then the saint, returning thanks, adored the Almighty Lord on bended knees; and rising from prayer he blessed that place and its surroundings in the name of the Lord. The boar, seeing what was done, came near, and by his frequent grunts seemed to ask something of the bishop: then the saint, scratching the head of the brute, and stroking his mouth and teeth, said:

"God Almighty, in Whose power are all the beasts of the forest, the oxen, the birds of the air, and the fishes of the sea, grant thee for thy conduct such reward as He knoweth is best for thee."

Then the boar, as if well remunerated, bowing his head to the priest of the Lord, departed, and betook himself to his well-known groves.

On the following night, as Kentigern lifted up his hands in the sanctuary, and blessed the Lord, it was revealed to him from on high that he was to inhabit that place, and there construct a monastery. In the morning he revealed to others the divine oracle that had been shown to him, and cheered on the souls of those who heard him to set about building.

For like bees making honey they toiled diligently at the work. Some cleared and levelled the site; others began to prepare the foundation of the ground; some cutting down trees, others carrying them, and others fitting them together, commenced, as the father had measured and marked out for them, to build a church and its offices of polished wood, after the fashion of the Britons, seeing that they could not yet build of stone, nor were accustomed to do so.

While they were hard at work, and the building was increasing, there came a heathen prince, Melconde Galganu by name, with his soldiers. The man, fierce and ignorant of God, with angry indignation demanded who they were, and how they had dared to do all this upon his land.

The saint, humbly replying to the interrogation, answered that they were Christians from the northern parts of Britain, that they had come thither to serve the living and true God. He asserted that he had begun the mansion there by the permission of King Cathwallain, his master, in whose possession he believed the place to be.

But he, furious and raging, ordered them all to be expelled from the place, and that whatever had been built should be pulled down and scattered; and so he began to return to his own home. And behold the hand of the Lord in chastisement touched him, and he was smitten with a sudden blindness. And yet, as was clear in the end, this did not happen to no good purpose, for inwardly enlightened, he caused himself to be carried to

the man of God, and began to entreat that by his
prayers he would dispel the darkness, and wash
him in the font of salvation.

The saint, who endeavoured to overcome evil
by good, willed to return to the man good for
evil; so after beginning with prayer, he laid his
healing hand on the blinded man in the name of
the Lord, and signing him with the cross of
salvation, turned his night into day. No sooner
therefore was he restored to sight than he was
dipped by the holy bishop in the saving water,
and henceforward he became an active and devoted fellow-worker in all that he desired at his
hand.

Taking an account of all his possessions, he
bestowed them on St Kentigern for the construc-
tion of his monastery, and, aided by this assistance,
he rapidly brought what he had commenced to
perfection. He established the Cathedral Chair of
his bishopric in the church of that monastery.

How his monastery flourished, and how the holy boy
Asaph carried fire without injuring himself.
There flocked to the monastery old and young,
rich and poor, to take upon themselves the easy
yoke and the light burden of the Lord. Nobles

and men of the middle class brought to the saint
their children to be trained unto the Lord. Among
them was one Asaph by name, distinguished by
birth and by looks, shining forth in virtue and
miracles from the flower of his first youth. He
sought to follow the life and teaching of his
master, as the reader of a little book of his Life
may learn at greater length, from which I have
thought fit to insert into this work one miracle,
because the perfection of the disciple is the glory
of the master.

Once upon a time in winter, when the frost
had congealed everything, St Kentigern, according to his custom, had recited the Psalter in the
coldest water, naked, and having resumed his
clothes and gone out in public, he began to be
oppressed by the cold and become entirely rigid.

Wherefore the holy father ordered the boy
Asaph to bring fire to him to warm himself. The
little boy ran to the oven and requested that coals
might be given to him. And when he had not
anything to carry the burning coals, the servant,
either in jest or seriously, said to him:

"If thou wishest to take the coals, hold out thy
tunic, for I have nothing at hand in which thou
mayest carry them."

The holy boy, without hesitation, gathering together and holding up his tunic, received the living coals in his bosom, and carrying them to the old man, cast them down in his presence. But no sign of burning or corruption appeared in the boy's clothing, whereupon the greatest astonishment seized all those who beheld it.

Holy Kentigern, who had always held dear and beloved the boy Asaph, henceforward regarded him as the dearest and most loved of all, and raised him as soon as he could to holy orders.

How St Kentigern went seven times to Rome, and consulted the blessed Gregory about his condition.

The blessed Kentigern, knowing that in many provinces of Britain the Church of God was in many ways reft and torn by idolaters from the faith of Christ; moreover that it was frequently assaulted by heretics, and that there were therein many things contrary to sound doctrine, and alien to the faith of our holy mother the Catholic Church, set himself for a long time to deliberate what cure to apply to all these evils.

In the end, he determined to visit the seat of Peter and he resolved by the wholesome teaching of the Holy Roman Church and by acknowledging the oracles of the faith, to cast out every scruple of doubt from his mind, so as to be able to arrive at the light of the truth. For Britain, during the reign of the most holy king Lucius, in the papacy of Eleutherius, by the preaching of the most excellent teachers Fagallus and Divianus and others, whom Gildas the wise, the historian of the Britons, commemorates, received the faith of Christ. It preserved that Christianity thus received whole and undefiled till the time of the Emperor Diocletian. Then the moon was turned into blood, and the flame of persecution against the Christians burnt brightly through the whole world. Then that scourge, inundating Britain, vehemently oppressed it, and pagan hands, mowing the first-fruits of the island, namely, Alban, took him to be recorded in the Book of the Eternal King; and an innumerable company of others shortly after.

From that time the worship of idols began to spring up, bringing in rejection and forgetfulness of the divine law. But Christianity after this somehow revived and flourished; however, time went on, and first the Pelagian heresy prevailing, and then the Arian creeping in, defiled the face of the Catholic faith which, however, sprang up again and flourished when these heresies were cast down and conquered by St Germanus, Bishop of Auxerre, a man truly apostolic, and made glorious by many miracles.

Yet forthwith the invasion of the neighbouring Picts and Scots, hostile to the name of Christ, drove away both the faith and the faithful from the northern part of Britain. Finally, Britain was conquered by the Angles, still pagans, from whom it was called Anglia. The natives being driven out, it was given over to idols and idolaters. The indigenous inhabitants of the island fled either across the sea into Little Britain, or into Wales, and though banished from their own land, all of them did not entirely abandon their faith.

But the Picts, first mainly by St Ninian, and then latterly by St Kentigern and St Columba, received the faith. Then having lapsed into apostasy a second time, by the preaching of St Kentigern, not only the Picts but also the Scots and innumerable people from the different parts of Britain, were either turned to the faith or were confirmed therein.

However, holy Augustine, noted for his monastic life and habit, and other servants of God, were sent to England by the most holy Pope Gregory, who converted the whole island to Christ, and fully instructed them in the rules of faith and the institutes of the holy fathers.

On account therefore of Britain being crushed by so many misfortunes, Christianity so often obscured, and even cast down, at different times diverse rites were found in her contrary to the form of the holy Roman Church and to the decrees of the holy fathers. In order that he might learn and be able to remedy all these evils, blessed Kentigern betook himself seven times to Rome, and brought home what he learned there, in so far as the correction of Britain required it; but as he was returning for the seventh time he was attacked by a most grievous malady, and got home with the greatest difficulty.

One of his visits was made to Rome during the time that blessed Gregory presided on the apostolic seat, a man truly apostolic in office, authority, life, and doctrine, and the special apostle of England, for the English are the sign of his apostleship.

Holy Bishop Kentigern, having received the apostolic absolution and benediction, returned home, bearing with him the codes of canons, many other books of Holy Scriptures, as well as privileges, and relics of the saints and ornaments of the Church, and whatever lends grace to the house of the Lord.

How holy Rederich invited St Kentigern to return to Glasgow; and how the holy prelate assented to the king's petition.

After the man of God had yielded to malice and departed, his enemies were not long permitted to triumph over his absence. For the Lord visited them with heavy hand and hard arm, smiting them with cruel chastisement, even to destruction.

But when the time of mercy had arrived, that the Lord might remove the rod of His fierce anger, and that they should turn unto Him, He raised up over the Cambrian kingdom a king, Rederech by name, who having been baptized in Ireland by the disciples of St Patrick, sought the Lord with all his heart, and strove to restore Christianity.

Wherefore King Rederech, seeing that the Christian religion was almost entirely destroyed in his kingdom, set himself zealously to restore it. And after long considering the matter in his own mind, and taking advice with other Christians who were in his confidence, he discovered no more healthful plan by which he could bring it to a successful result, than to send messengers to St Kentigern to recall him to his first see.

On receiving them, the holy father was silent, nor did he return any definite answer, for he had prepared to end his days in that glorious monastery which he had raised with long and great labour.

And while on the following night he was engaged in prayer, the angel of the Lord stood beside him, and said unto him:

"Go back to Glasgow, to thy church, and there thou shalt truly acquire unto the Lord thy God a holy nation, and thou shalt receive an everlasting crown from Him. There thou shalt end thy days in a good old age, and shall go out of this world unto thy Father which is in heaven."

Having said this, the angel departed; but Kentigern gave thanks to the Lord, saying:

"My heart is ready, O God! My heart is ready for whatever may please Thee."

How the saint, addressing his disciples about his return, appointed St Asaph as his successor.

And when the day dawned, having called his disciples together, he said to them:

"Dearly beloved, it is laid upon me by the Lord that I should return to my own church of Glasgow; nor will we contradict the words of the Holy One, as Job saith; but rather in all things obey His will and command, even to our life's end.

"Do you, therefore, most beloved ones, stand firm in the faith. Acquit you like men and be comforted, and seek always that everything be done in charity."

These, and many such things, he said in their presence, and lifting his hand he blessed them. Then he appointed St Asaph to the government of the monastery and as the successor of his bishopric.

Of that monastery, a great part of the brethren, to the number of six hundred and sixty-five, in no way being able or willing to live without him so long as he survived, went away with him. Three hundred only abode with St Asaph.

When King Rederech and his people heard that Kentigern had arrived from Wales into Cambria, from exile into his own country, with great joy and peace both king and people went out to meet him.

*Of the devils miraculously driven away, and of the place
where he stood to preach, and of the fertility of the land
which ensued.*

Blessed Kentigern, on seeing the approach of a
great multitude hastening towards him, rejoiced
in spirit, and offering up thanks, he knelt down
in prayer. Then he arose and, in the Name of the
Holy Trinity, blessed the assembled multitude.

Whereupon, an immense number of phan-
toms, horrible in appearance, coming out of that
crowd, fled away in the sight of all; and a great
terror fell on those who beheld them. The holy
bishop, comforting them and strengthening them,
laid bare the nature of those in whom they had
believed, and encouraged all who stood around
to believe in the living God.

And when he had finished his teaching, the
ground on which he sat, in a place which is called
Holdelm, in the sight of all grew into a little hill,
and remains there to this day.

After the inhabitants of Cambria had turned
to the Lord and were baptized, all the elements,
which in vindication of the divine justice had
seemed leagued for its ruin, put on a new face.
For by the Lord causing His face to shine upon
them, the sun was felt warmer than usual, the

vault of heaven clearer, the air more healthy, the earth more fruitful, the sea more calm, and the abundance of all things greater.

How King Rederech conceded to him power over himself and his posterity.

Now King Rederech was filled with great joy. And he made no delay in exhibiting the fervour which animated his soul. For, stripping himself of his royal robes, on bended knees and hands joined, he gave his homage to St Kentigern, and handed over to him the dominion and princedom over all his kingdom, and willed that he should be king, and himself the ruler of his country under him as his father, as he knew that formerly the great Emperor Constantine had done to St Silvester.

St Kentigern did not hesitate to accept what the king had so devoutly offered, because he foresaw that this would be for the advantage of the Church. He had also a privilege from the Supreme Pontiff, that he should be subject to no bishop, but rather should be styled the vicar and chaplain of the Pope.

Moreover, Rederech's queen Languoreth, long bowed down by the disgrace of barrenness, by the blessing and intercession of the saintly bishop, conceived and brought forth a son; and the saint baptizing him, called him Constantine, in remembrance of the act of his father which he had done to him in resemblance of that which the Roman Emperor Constantine had done to St Silvester.

The holy bishop Kentigern, building churches in Holdelm, ordaining priests and clerics, placed his see there for a time; afterwards, warned by divine revelation, he transferred it to his own city Glasgow.

How the saint miraculously restored to the queen the ring which she had improperly given away.

Queen Languoreth, living in plenty and delights, was not faithful to the royal chamber or the marital bed, as she ought to have been: for the wealth of her treasures, the exuberance of her means of sensuality, and the elevation of power, gave incentives and fuel to the will of the flesh. She cast her eyes on a certain youth, a soldier, who seemed to her to be beautiful and fair of aspect beyond many at court. And he, who without external temptation, was himself ready enough for such a service as this, was easily induced to sin with her.

As time passed, the forbidden pleasures, frequently repeated, became more and more delightful to both of them; so from a rash act they proceeded to a blind love, and a royal ring of gold, set with a precious gem, which her lawful husband had entrusted to her as a special mark of his conjugal love, she very imprudently bestowed upon her lover. He, more impudently and more imprudently placing it upon his finger, opened the door of suspicion to all who were conversant in the matter.

A faithful servant of the king, finding this out, took care to instil the secret of the queen and the soldier into the ears of the husband, who did not willingly lend his ear or his mind to her disgrace. But the detector of the adultery, in proof of the matter, showed the ring on the finger of the soldier; and so persuading the king to believe him, he succeeded in kindling the spirit of jealousy within him.

The king veiled under a calm demeanour his wrath against the queen and the soldier, and appeared more than usually cheerful and kind. But when a bright day occurred, he went out hunting, and summoning the soldier to accompany him, sought the woods and forests with a great company of beaters and dogs. Having loosed the dogs and stationed his friends at different places, the king with the soldier came down to the banks of the river Clud, and they, in a shady place on the green turf, thought it would be pleasant to sleep for a little.

The soldier, suspecting no danger and resting his head, straightaway slumbered; but the spirit of jealousy exciting the king, suffered him neither to slumber nor to take any rest. Seeing the ring on the finger of the sleeper, his wrath was kindled, and he with difficulty restrained his hand from his sword and from shedding of blood; but he controlled his rage, and after drawing the ring off the finger threw it into the river, and then, waking the man, ordered him to return to his companions and go home. The soldier waking up from sleep, and thinking nothing about the ring, obeyed the king's order, and never discovered what he had lost till he entered his house.

But when, on the return of the king, the queen in the usual manner came forth from her chamber and saluted him, from his mouth there proceeded threats, contempt, and reproach, while with flashing eyes and menacing countenance he demanded where the ring was which he had entrusted to her keeping. When she declared that she had it laid up in a casket, the king, in the presence of all his courtiers, commanded her to bring it to him. She, still full of hope, entered the inner chamber as if to seek the ring, but straightaway sent a messenger to the soldier, telling him of the king's anger, and ordering him to send the ring back quickly.

The soldier sent back to the queen to say that he had lost the ring and could not tell where. Then, fearing the face of the king, for the sake of concealment, he absented himself from court. In the meantime, as she sought further delays, and was slow in producing what, of course, she could not find, uselessly seeking here and there, the king in fury frequently calling her an adulteress, broke forth in curses saying:

"God do to me, and more also, if I judge thee not according to the law of adulterers, and condemn thee to a most disgraceful death. Thou, clinging to a young adulterer, hast neglected the king thy spouse; yet I would have made thee the sharer of my bed and the mistress of my kingdom: thou hast done it in secret; I will do it in public, and the sun shall manifest thine ignominy and reveal thy more shameful things before thy face."

And when he had said much after this sort, all

the courtiers praying for some delay, he with difficulty conceded three days, and ordered her to be imprisoned. Cast into a dungeon, she now contemplated death as imminent; but not the less did her guilty conscience torment her.

By the inspiration of the Lord, the woman in her great strait sent a faithful messenger to St Kentigern, told him her whole misfortune, and urgently requested help. She also begged that at least he would use his influence with the king and beseech pardon for her, for there was nothing so great which he would, or could, or ought to deny him.

The saintly bishop, knowing the whole story before the arrival of the messenger, ordered him to go with a hook to the bank of the river Clud, to cast the hook into the stream, and to bring back to him straightaway the first fish that was caught upon it and taken out of the water.

The man did what the saint commanded, and exhibited in the presence of the man of God a large fish which is commonly called a salmon; and on his ordering it to be cut open and gutted in his presence, he found in it the ring in question, which he straightaway sent by the same messenger to the queen. And when she saw it and received it, her heart was filled with joy, her mouth with praise and thanksgiving.

Therefore the queen returned to the king the ring he had required, in the sight of all. Wherefore the king and all his court were sorry for the injuries done to the queen; and humbly on his knees he sought her pardon, and swore that he would inflict a severe punishment, even death or exile if she willed, upon her slanderers. But she wisely desired that he should show mercy. And so the king, and the queen, and the accuser were recalled to the grace of peace and mutual love.

How a jester despising the gifts of the king demanded a dishful of fresh mulberries after Christmas; and received them through St Kentigern.

A jester from one of the kings of Ireland, skilled and clever in his art, was sent to Cambria to the court of the king, that he might see whether the truth responded to the fame of his generosity, which was far and wide extended.

The jester, admitted into the court, played on the timbrel and harp, and gave joy to the king and his paladins all the days of the Christmas holidays. When the feast of the Lord's holy Epiphany was past, the king ordered gifts to be brought forth

and bestowed upon the jester, in accordance with
the royal generosity, all of which the actor refused,
stating that he had sufficiency of such things in
his own country.

Being asked by the king what he would be
willing to receive, he answered that he had no
need whatever of silver, and gold, and garments,
and horses, in which Ireland abounded; but "if
thou desirest," said he, "that I should depart from
thee well rewarded, let there be given to me a dish
full of fresh mulberries."

When they heard this speech uttered from the
mouth of the man, all burst out laughing, because
they thought that he was joking and speaking in
sport. But he with an oath declared that he had
demanded the mulberries not in jest but in all
seriousness; nor could he be moved from this by
prayers, promises, or the offer of the handsomest
gifts; and rising, he declared that he wished to
retire from the midst of the crowd, and, as the
saying, is, to carry off the king's honour.

The king took this very ill, and asked his
companions what could be done that he should
not be dishonoured in this matter; for it was the
season of winter and not a mulberry could be
found anywhere. Acting on the advice of his

courtiers, he betook himself to St Kentigern, and
humbly begged that by prayer he would obtain
what he wanted from God. The man of God,
although he thought that his prayer would not be
fitly offered for such trifles as these, knowing that
the king had a great devotion to God and Holy
Church, made up his mind to condescend to his
petition, hoping that thereby in the future he
might advance in virtue.

Therefore pondering for a time in his heart,
and praying shortly, he said to the king:

"Dost thou remember in what place during
summer, thou didst throw away thy garment in
the great heat when hunting, that thou mightest
follow the dogs more expeditiously, and then
thou didst never return to recover what thou
hadst cast off?"

The king answered, saying: "I know, my lord
and bishop, both the time and the place."

"Go straightaway to the place, " said the saint,
"and thou shalt find the garment still hanging
over a bush of thorns, and below that thou shalt
find mulberries still fresh and fit for gathering.
Take them and satisfy the demand of the jester,
and in all things concern thyself that thou more
and more reverence God, who will not allow

thine honour to be diminished even in so light a thing as this."

The king did as the bishop ordered, and found all as he had predicted. Therefore taking the dish and filling it with the mulberries, he gave it to the actor who, seeing the charger full of mulberries contrary to the time of the year, wondered and feared, and when he knew how it had happened, he cried out and said:

"Indeed, there is none like thee among the kings of the earth, munificent in thy generosity, and there is none like Kentigern, glorious in holiness, fearful in praises, doing such wonders in my sight beyond expectation. Henceforth I will not leave thy house or thy service, and I will be to thee a servant for ever, so long as I live."

The actor therefore abode in the king's court, and served him for many days as jester. Afterwards, by the instigation of the fear of God, he set himself against his former profession, renounced the trade of actor, and entering the ways of a better life, gave himself up to the service of God.

How St Columba visited blessed Kentigern, and beheld a crown that came down from heaven upon his head.
St Columba, the abbot, whom the Angles call

Colum-cille, a man wonderful for doctrine and
virtues, full of the spirit of prophecy, was living in
that glorious monastery which he had erected in
the island of Yi (Iona). He desired earnestly to
approach the holy Kentigern, to visit him, to
behold him, to come into his close intimacy, and
to consult him regarding the things which lay
near his own heart.

And when the proper time came the holy
father St Columba went forth, and a great company of his disciples and others who desired to
behold the face of so great a man, accompanied
him. When he approached the place called Mellingdenor, where the saint abode at that time, he
divided all his people into three bands, and sent
forward a message to announce to the holy prelate his arrival.

The holy pontiff was glad, and calling together
his clergy and people similarly in three bands, he
went forth to meet them, singing spiritual songs.

On St Columba's side, some who had come
with St Columba asked him, saying: "Hath St
Kentigern come in the first chorus of singers?"

The saint answered: "Neither in the first nor
in the second cometh the gentle saint."

And when they asked how he knew this, he

said: "I see a fiery pillar fashioned like a golden crown, set with sparkling gems, descending from heaven upon his head, and a light of heavenly brightness encircling him like a veil, and covering him, and again returning to the skies. Wherefore it is given to me to know by this sign that, like Aaron, he is the elect of God, and sanctified; who, clothed with light as with a garment, and with a golden crown represented on his head appeareth to me with the sign of sanctity."

When these two godlike men met, they mutually embraced and kissed each other, and having first satiated themselves with divine words, they refreshed themselves with bodily food.

How Kentigern erected crosses in many places, by which, even to the present day, miracles are wrought.

The venerable Kentigern had a custom, in the places in which at any time he had won the people to the dominion of Christ, or had dwelt for any length of time, there to erect the triumphant standard of the cross.

Among many crosses which he erected where the word of the Lord was preached, he erected two which to the present time work miracles. One in his own city of Glasgow he caused to be

cut by quarriers from a block of stone of wondrous size, which, by the united exertions of many
men, and by the application of machinery, he
ordered to be erected in the cemetery of the
church of the Holy Trinity, in which his episcopal
chair was placed. But all their labour was ex-
pended in vain; every machine was powerless,
human strength and might availed not to raise it
up.

But when human genius and help failed, the
saint had recourse to divine aid. For on the
succeeding night, an angel of the Lord descended
from heaven and coming near, rolled back the
stone cross and raised it to the place where it
stands today.

The people, when they came to the church in
the morning and saw what was done, were astonished and gave glory to God. For the cross was
very large, and never from that time lacked great
virtue, seeing that many maniacs and those vexed
with unclean spirits are used to be tied of a
Sunday night to that cross, and in the morning
they are found restored, freed, and cleansed,
though often they are found dead or at the point
of death.

How he tied up his chin with a bandage, and how he prepared for his soul's departure.

Blessed Kentigern, overcome by old age, perceived from many cracks in it that the ruin of his earthly house was imminent; but the foundation of his faith, which was founded on the Rock, comforted his soul.

And because of the extremity of old age and infirmity, the fastenings of his nerves were almost entirely withered and loosened, therefore he bound up his cheeks and his chin by a certain linen bandage, which went over his head and under his chin, neither too tight nor too loose. This the most refined man did, that by the fall of his chin nothing indecent should appear in the gaping of his mouth.

In the end this man, beloved by God and man, knowing that the hour was drawing near when he should pass out of this world, fortified himself with the sacred unction and with the life-giving sacraments. He warned his disciples, gathered around him, so far as his strength would allow him, concerning the observance of the holy rule, the maintenance of love and peace, of the grace of hospitality, and of prayer and holy study.

After that, he gave to each of them, as they

humbly knelt before him, the kiss of peace; and lifting his hand as best he could, he blessed them, and bidding them his last farewell, he committed them all to the guardianship of the Holy Trinity, and to the protection of the holy Mother of God, and gathered himself up into his stone bed. Then one voice of mourners sounded full everywhere, and a horror of confusion fell on the faces of all of them.

Of his disciples who sought a speedy journey to heaven, and of his warm bath.
Some of them, who very dearly loved the saint of God, besought him thus:

"O Lord Bishop, thou desirest to depart and to be with Christ; but, we pray thee, have mercy upon us whom thou hast begotten in Christ. Since we have no power of retaining thee longer among us, pray to the Lord that to grant to us to depart with thee from this vale of tears to the glory of thy Lord."

And when they had urged him more with tears, the man of God, full of compassion, collecting his breath as best he might, said: "The will of the Lord be done in us all: and do with us as He best knoweth, and as is well-pleasing unto Him."

After these things the saint was silent, and sighing in his soul for heaven, he awaited the passage of his spirit from the body; and his disciples watching by him, took care of him as if close to death. And behold, while the morning day-star shone forth, an angel of the Lord appeared with unspeakable splendour, and the glory of God shone around him. And for fear of him the guardians of the holy bishop were astonished and amazed and, unable to bear so great glory, became as dead men.

But the holy old man, comforted by the angelic vision, held close converse with the angel as with his closest and dearest friend.

Now the heavenly messenger said to him:

"Kentigern, chosen and beloved of God, rejoice and be glad. Thy prayer is heard, and the divine ear hath listened to the preparation of thy heart. It shall be to thy disciples who desire to accompany thee as thou willest.

"And because thy whole life in this world hath been a continual martyrdom, it hath pleased the Lord that thy mode of leaving it shall be easier than that of other men. Cause, therefore, on the morrow that a warm bath be prepared for thee, and entering therein, thou shalt fall asleep in the

Lord without pain, and take thy quiet rest in Him.
And even before the water hath begun to cool
but is yet warm about thee, let thy brethren follow
thee into the bath, and straightaway, loosed from
the bonds of death, they shall migrate as companions of thy journey, and with thee enter into the
joy of the Lord."

With these words the angelic vision and voice
departed; but a wondrous fragrance filled the
place and all that were therein. And the holy man,
calling together his disciples, revealed to them the
secret of the angel, and ordered that his bath
should be prepared as the Lord commanded by
his messenger.

*How he passed out of this world, and how he shone
forth after his death in many miracles.*
When the octave of the Lord's Epiphany, on
which the gentle bishop had been wont every
year to baptize a multitude of people, was dawn-
ing — a day very acceptable to St Kentigern and
to the sons of his adoption — the holy man, borne
by their hands, entered a bath filled with hot
water, which he first blessed with the sign of
salvation.

And when the saint had been some little time

in it, after lifting his hands and his eyes to heaven, and bowing his head as if sinking into a calm sleep, he yielded up his spirit. For he seemed as free from the pain of death as he stood forth spotless and pure from the corruption of the flesh and the snares of this world.

The disciples lifted the holy body out of the bath, and eagerly strove with each other to enter the water; and so, one by one, before the water cooled they slept in the Lord in great peace, and having tasted death along with their holy bishop, they entered with him into the mansions of heaven.

The brethren stripped the saint of his ordinary clothes, which they partly reserved and partly distributed as precious relics, and clothed him in the consecrated garments which became so great a bishop. Then he was carried by the brethren into the choir with chants and psalms, and the life-giving Victim was offered to God for him by many. Diligently and most devoutly as the custom of the Church in those days demanded, they celebrated his funeral; and on the right side of the altar they laid beneath a stone, with as much reverence as they could, that abode of virtues. The sacred remains of all these brethren were devoutly consigned to the cemetery for burial, in the order in which they had followed the holy bishop out of this life.

Thus blessed Kentigern, when he was one hundred and eighty-five years old, famous for signs, wonders and prophecies, left this world and went to the Father.

The spirit of St Kentigern being taken up to the starry realms, that which the Earth had bestowed she gathered into her womb. But the power of miracles which had existed in him when alive now burst forth. At his tomb sight is restored to the blind, hearing to the deaf, the power of walking to the lame, strength of limb to the paralytic, a sound mind to the insane, speech to the dumb, cleanness of skin to the lepers.

Of the prophecy of a certain man, and of the burial of the saints in Glasgow.
In the same year that St Kentigern migrated to the heavens, King Rederech remained much longer than usual in the royal town, which was called Pertnech. In his court there lived a fool called Laloecen, who was in the habit of receiving the necessaries of food and clothing from the munificence of the king.

This man, after the death of St Kentigern, gave himself up to the most extreme grief, and would receive no consolation from anyone. When they asked him why he mourned so inconsolably, he answered that his lord, King Rederech, and another of the chiefs of the land, by name Morthec, would not live long after the death of the holy bishop. That the saying of the fool was uttered prophetically, was clearly proved by the fact that both king and prince died in the same year, and were buried in Glasgow.

Here ends the Life of the most holy Kentigern, Bishop and Confessor, who is also called Mungo.